I want Jesus to be the central reality of my life.

Copyright

Can Prayer Change Your Life?: 12 Powerful Biblical Prayers For Spiritual Growth, by Stephen H Berkey, published by Get Wisdom Publishing, Box 465, Thompsons Station, TN 37179, copyright © 2026, Stephen H Berkey.
Printed in the United States of America

All rights reserved. No portion of this book may be reproduced in any form without written permission from the publisher, except as permitted by U.S. copyright law. For permission contact: info@getwisdompublishing.com

Scriptures marked NIV are taken from the NEW INTERNATIONAL VERSION (NIV): Scripture taken from THE HOLY BIBLE, NEW INTERNATIONAL VERSION ®. Copyright© 1973, 1978, 1984, 2011 by Biblica, Inc.™. Used by permission of Zondervan

Scriptures without a marked translation are generally based on the NIV, NLT, and HCSB translations.

ISBN 978-1-952359-81-1 (paperback)
ISBN 978-1-952359-82-8 (ebook)
Audiobook available(Amazon.com and audible.com)

For more information about Get Wisdom Publishing: https://getwisdompublishing.com/

The Wisdom Prayer Series

Can Prayer Change Your Life?

12 Powerful Biblical Prayers For Spiritual Growth

Stephen H Berkey

Free PDF

Life Improvement Principles

[Get the ebook version for 99 cents]

You can live your best life!

Welcome to a journey of discovery! In case you have forgotten, your actions have consequences. Unlock your potential! This book (60+ pages) provides the overview of all our strategies and wisdom principles to live your best life. You *can* transform your life! Get your wisdom-based roadmap to a better life and unlock all the possibilities for growth and success.

Free PDF: https://getwisdompublishing.com/resource-registration/

Kindle ebook for 99 cents:
https://www.amazon.com/dp/B0FG883KZM

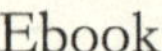

Free PDF

Make it your life goal to be the best you can be!

Discover Wisdom and live the life you deserve.

Table of Contents

How To Use This Book

This book is designed to help you pray in a way that transforms your life. Not just to say words—but to experience real change.

Each section focuses on one important area of spiritual growth. These topics reflect the kind of prayers found throughout Scripture—prayers that align your heart with God and guide your life in the right direction.

You will not need a lot of time to use this book. But you will need intention. This book is not meant to be rushed. It is meant to be returned to—again and again—until the prayers begin to take root in your thinking, your choices, and your daily life.

Each section follows a repeatable pattern:

- A key transformational prayer
- A Scripture to anchor your understanding
- Additional prayers you can use immediately
- Reflection to apply what you are praying
- A practical step to guide your day

You can move through the book in different ways. You may choose to work through one section at a time. You may stay with a single prayer for several days. You may return to a section that speaks directly to your current situation.

There is no single "right" pace. The goal is not to finish quickly. The goal is to let the prayers shape your life. Keep a few simple principles in mind:

<u>First, keep your prayers honest.</u>
You do not need perfect words. You can begin with the prayers on the page, but make them your own as you go.

<u>Second, keep your focus clear.</u>
Each section centers on one key idea. Stay with that idea long enough for it to move from your mind to your heart.

<u>Third, keep your practice consistent.</u>
Small, repeated regular moments of prayer will shape your life more than long occasional efforts.

Over time, something important happens:

- You will notice your thoughts changing.
- Your responses will become steadier.
- Your perspective will become clearer.

The prayers will begin to move from the page to your daily life. And that is the purpose of this book. If you stay with it, you will say the prayers and . . . begin to live them.

Note To The Reader

Most people want a stronger spiritual life. They want to know God personally. That means trusting Him more fully while living with greater clarity and purpose. But knowing how to grow in these areas is not always obvious:

- You may already believe.
- You may already pray.
- You may already desire something deeper.

Yet, something still feels incomplete. This book was written for that space. It is built on a simple concept: The prayers you pray shape your lifestyle and the life you live.

Throughout Scripture the most meaningful prayers are not long or complicated. They are focused and aligned with God's truth. They speak to what matters and mold the person who prays them.

This book brings together a set of those kinds of prayers—prayer that form your thinking and deepen your relationship with God.

You will not find long explanations here. You will not find complex instruction. Instead, you will find clear, simple prayers you can return to again and again.

Some of these prayers may feel natural to you. Others may challenge you. That is part of the process. Growth rarely happens all at once. It happens gradually as you return to what is true and allow it to take root.

You do not need to do this perfectly and you don't need to have everything figured out. You simply need a willing heart and a consistent prayer time.

If you stay with these prayers—if you return to them regularly—you will notice change. Not in a sudden or dramatic way, but in a steady and lasting lifestyle.

You will begin to think, respond, and live differently. As time passes that steady change becomes something much greater.

It becomes a life transformed by God. That is the invitation in these pages.

It is available to you, one prayer at a time.

Steve

SECTION 1

Knowing God

1
Transformational Prayer

Knowing God

Father,
I know about You, but I do not always know You personally.
I move through my days distracted and unaware of Your presence.
Slow me down and draw my attention back to You.
Open my heart so I can recognize You, respond to You, and walk with You more closely each day.
Amen.

Memory Prayer:
Lord, help me truly know You.

1
Transformational Prayer

Scripture

Ephesians 1:17–18

"...that you may know Him better...
that the eyes of your heart may
be enlightened..."

1
Why This Prayer Matters

Why is it possible to believe in God and still feel distant from Him? Many people know the right truths, yet something feels missing. There is a difference between knowing about God and actually knowing Him in a personal way.

Paul prayed for more than knowledge. He asked God to open the eyes of the heart, because real understanding comes through relationship, not just information. This kind of knowing cannot be forced—it is revealed as you seek His presence in your life.

When you begin to truly know God, your faith becomes personal and real. You start to recognize His presence in everyday moments. You will respond to Him more naturally. This prayer moves you into a closer relationship with Your God.

1
When to Pray This Prayer

Pray this when your faith feels distant or routine. When you know the truth but do not feel close to God, this prayer helps you return to relationship.

Pray this when you are reading Scripture but not sensing connection. Ask God to make His truth real to your heart, not just your mind.

Pray this at the start of your day. Before distractions take over, take a moment to seek Him intentionally and invite Him into your presence.

1

Let Me Dwell with You

Psalm 27:4

Lord,
Give me a desire to be with You.
Help me choose Your presence over distraction. Teach me to remain with You, not just visit You.
Let my heart find rest in You.
Amen.

Help Me Seek You Fully

Jeremiah 29:13

Father,
I want to seek You with my whole heart. Remove what divides my attention.
Give me a true desire to pursue You.
Help me keep seeking until I find You.
Amen.

1
Reflect and Respond

Do you feel close to God right now or does your faith feel distant? Take a moment and be honest about where you are.

What has been competing for your attention and pulling you away from time with Him? Identify one distraction you can set aside.

Choose one small step today to seek God more intentionally. Even a few focused moments can begin to restore your awareness of His presence.

1
Create a Hunger for You

Psalm 63:1

God,
Create in me a deep hunger for You. When I feel empty, remind me that You are what I need most. Draw my heart back to You again and again. Let my soul find satisfaction and rest in You.
Amen.

Help Me Know You Personally

Philippians 3:10

Lord Jesus,
I want to know You in a real and personal way. Let me experience Your presence in my life. Walk with me through both success and struggle. Help me grow closer to You each day.
Amen.

1
Reflect and Respond

Has your desire for God grown stronger or has it slowly faded? Be honest about what your heart is truly pursuing.

What would it look like for you to seek a more personal relationship with Christ today? Think of one specific way to move toward Him.

Ask God to renew your desire and draw you closer to Him. As you respond, your relationship with Him will become more real and meaningful.

1
Live This Today

Pause and pray before beginning one of your tasks today. Turn your attention to God. Quietly acknowledge His presence and invite Him to participate in your life at that moment.

You do not need perfect words or long prayers. God meets you in simple sincere moments. As you continue to turn toward Him, you will begin to recognize that He is already near and at work in your life.

SECTION 2

Loving God Fully

2
Transformational Prayer

Loving God Fully

Father,
I say I love You, but my attention is often divided.
Other things quietly take first place in my heart.
Gather my scattered desires and refocus them on You.
Teach me to love You fully—with all my thoughts and choices.
Amen.

Memory Prayer:
Lord, give me an undivided heart.

2
Transformational Prayer

Scripture

Matthew 22:37

"Love the Lord your God with all your heart… soul… and mind."

2
Why This Prayer Matters

What does it mean to love God fully—and why does it feel so difficult to do consistently? Most people intend to love God, but their attention is often divided by competing priorities.

Jesus made it clear that loving God is the greatest commandment. This is not just about belief—it is about where your heart must be centered. Love for God grows as you intentionally align your life with Him.

As your love deepens, your life begins to center on Him. Your decisions become clearer and your relationship with Him becomes more personal. This prayer helps move your love from intention to reality.

2
When to Pray This Prayer

Pray this prayer when your attention begins to drift away from God. When other activities begin to take priority, this prayer helps you return your focus to Him.

Pray when your faith feels routine instead of personal. Ask God to renew your desire so your relationship does not become mechanical.

Pray this before making decisions. Let your love for God shape your decisions and guide your life.

2
Let My Love Be Whole

Deuteronomy 6:5

Lord,
Teach me to love You with all that I am – with my thoughts, my desires, and my choices. Remove anything that divides my devotion to You. Let my whole life reflect my love for You.
Amen.

Unite My Heart

Psalm 86:11

Father,
Give me an undivided heart.
Remove the distractions that pull me in different directions. Help me focus totally on You. Prepare my heart to be steady and devoted to You alone.
Amen.

2
Reflect and Respond

What is currently competing for your attention and affection? Be clear and truthful about what has been taking first place in your life.

Does your love for God feel strong and central or distant and divided? Consider where your heart is truly focused today.

Choose one small way to turn your attention back to God. Even a simple shift can begin to realign your heart with His ways.

2
Create a Deep Longing

Psalm 42:1

God,
Let my heart long for You.
Create in me a deep desire to be near You. When I feel empty remind me that You are what I need. Draw me closer to You each day.
Amen.

Let Me Delight in You

Psalm 63:3–4

Lord,
Help me see Your love as better than anything else. I want to delight in You. Teach me to praise You and lift my thoughts toward You. Let my joy be found in knowing You.
Amen.

2
Reflect and Respond

Has your desire for God grown stronger or has it been replaced by other pursuits? Consider what your heart is truly seeking.

What would it look like to delight in God today, not just think about Him? Identify one simple way to turn your attention toward Him.

Ask God to renew your desire so your relationship with Him becomes more alive and meaningful.

2
Live This Today

Pause at least once today and intentionally turn your attention toward God. In the middle of your routines, acknowledge Him and choose Him over distraction.

Love for God will grow through small intentional choices. As you continue to turn your heart and mind toward Him your love will deepen and become more real and alive.

SECTION 3

Trusting God Completely

3
Transformational Prayer

Trusting God Completely

Father,
I say I trust You, but I still try to be the one in control.
When I feel uncertain I rely on my own understanding.
Help me release that desire for control.
Teach me to trust Your guidance, even when the path ahead is unclear.
Amen.

Memory Prayer:
Lord, I trust you – overcome my doubt.

3
Transformational Prayer

Scripture

Proverbs 3:5–6

"Trust in the Lord with all your heart…
and He will make your
paths straight."

3
Why This Prayer Matters

Trust sounds simple and easy until life becomes uncertain. When you cannot see what is ahead, your instinct is often to rely on what feels comfortable.

God calls you to something deeper. He invites you to trust Him fully, not only when things are clear, but especially when they are not. This kind of trust shifts your confidence away from your understanding and toward His.

As you learn to trust God anxiety will begin to loosen its grip. You will move forward with confidence because you will know He is guiding you. This prayer helps you release control and rely on His direction.

3
When to Pray This Prayer

Pray this when you feel uncertain about what to do next. When the path ahead is unclear this prayer helps you focus on God instead of your own thoughts and understanding.

Pray this when anxiety begins to rise. When your thoughts feel unsettled, bring them honestly to God and ask Him to steady your heart.

Pray this when you are trying to control outcomes. When letting go feels difficult this prayer helps you give up what you cannot manage.

3
I Commit My Way to You

Psalm 37:5

Lord,
I place my plans and my path in Your hands. Help me trust You with what lies ahead. Guide my steps and establish what is right. Teach me to rest in Your ways.
Amen.

I Bring You My Worries

Philippians 4:6–7

Father,
I bring my concerns to You instead of carrying them alone. When anxiety rises remind me that You are near.
Guard my heart and mind with Your peace. Help me trust You with what I cannot control.
Amen.

3
Reflect and Respond

What situation in your life feels most uncertain right now? Identify where you are struggling to trust God.

Are you trying to control something that is beyond your ability to manage? Be honest about where you are holding on too tightly.

Bring that situation before God today. Ask Him to help you release your control and trust His guidance, one step at a time.

3
When I Am Afraid, I Trust You

Psalm 56:3–4

God,
When fear rises help me turn to You first. Remind me that You are greater than what I face. Strengthen my heart so I trust You in uncertain moments. Let my confidence rest in You.
Amen.

Help My Unbelief

Mark 9:24

Lord,
I want to trust You, but I struggle. Meet me in my doubt and strengthen my faith. Do not let uncertainty pull me away from You. Teach me to trust You more fully each day.
Amen.

3
Reflect and Respond

Does fear or doubt tend to guide your reactions more than trust? Notice how you tend to respond under pressure.

Where do you need to trust God more deeply right now? Be specific.

Ask Him to meet you in both your assurance and your doubt or unbelief. He is able to strengthen your trust, even in uncertain moments.

3
Live This Today

Pause before one of your significant decisions or concerns today and consciously place it in God's hands. Choose to trust Him instead of trying to control the outcome.

You do not need perfect clarity to trust God. As you take small steps of surrender, you will begin to see that He is steady, faithful, and able to guide your life.

SECTION 4

Surrendering to God

4
Transformational Prayer

Surrendering to God

Father,
I want Your will but I still cling to my own plans.
When Your direction feels difficult I resist letting go.
Soften the stubbornness within me.
Help me release control and follow You fully—even in those times when it costs me something.
Amen.

Memory Prayer:
Not my will, but Yours be done.

4
Transformational Prayer

Scripture

Luke 22:42

"Father, if You are willing…
not my will, but Yours be done."

4
Why This Prayer Matters

Surrender often sounds right—but it feels difficult. You may want God's direction, yet still prefer your own plan when it comes down to a real decision.

Letting go can feel like losing control, but in reality it's choosing to trust God's wisdom over your own. Jesus faced this moment and chose the Father's will, even when it was costly.

When you begin to surrender, you stop carrying the weight of trying to control everything. You experience God's direction and peace in a deeper way. This prayer helps you align your life with His will.

4
When to Pray This Prayer

Pray this when you feel resistance to what God is leading you to do. When you want your way more than His, this prayer helps you realign your heart.

Pray this when your plans are not unfolding as you expected. When circumstances change, surrender will help you trust God's purpose.

Pray this when you are holding tightly to control. When letting go feels difficult, this prayer helps you release your grip.

4
I Offer My Life to You

Romans 12:1

Lord,
I offer my life to You. My thoughts and my actions belong to You.
Transform me according to Your purposes. Help me live in a way that honors You.
Amen.

Teach Me to Do Your Will

Psalm 143:10

Father,
Teach me to follow Your ways.
Lead me in what is right and true.
Guide my steps so I walk in obedience.
Let Your Spirit direct my life.
Amen.

4
Reflect and Respond

Where are you resisting God right now? Identify a specific area where surrender feels difficult.

What are you holding onto that needs to be released? Be real about your desire for control.

Bring that area before God today. Ask Him to help you trust His direction and give you the courage to follow.

4
I Live Through You

Galatians 2:20

Lord Jesus,
My life is no longer my own.
Live through me in all I do.
Direct my plans and my actions.
Help me follow You daily.
Amen.

Your Will Be Done

Matthew 6:10

Father,
Let Your will be done in my life.
Align my heart with Your purposes.
Help me trust Your plans above my own. Lead me in the way You have already prepared for me.
Amen.

4
Reflect and Respond

Do you see surrender as something to resist or something to trust? Consider how your perspective affects your response to God.

Where do you need to let go today? Identify one specific area.

Ask God to help you trust that His plans are good. As you accept His ways, He will guide you with wisdom and His love and care.

4
Live This Today

Identify one situation in your life today where you are holding onto control. Pause and consciously release it to God, choosing His will over your own.

Surrender is not losing—it is trusting God with what matters most. As you take small steps of obedience, you will begin to experience His peace and direction more clearly.

SECTION 5

Seeking God's Wisdom

5
Transformational Prayer

Seeking God's Wisdom

Father,
I often make decisions too quickly,
relying on what I think is right.
I move ahead without truly seeking
Your guidance.
Slow me down and clear my thinking.
Give me wisdom that comes from You
and help me follow it with confidence.
Amen.

Memory Prayer:
Lord, give me Your wisdom.

5
Transformational Prayer

Scripture

James 1:5

"If any of you lacks wisdom…
it will be given to you."

5
Why This Prayer Matters

Most decisions are made quickly, often based on habit or instinct. In the moment it feels easier to rely on your own thinking than to pause and seek God's direction.

But your understanding is limited. What seems right in the moment may not lead where you expect. God offers something better—wisdom that brings clarity and understanding based on His knowledge and perspective.

When you begin to seek God's wisdom, your decisions become more grounded and intentional. You are no longer guessing. You are being guided by Almighty God. This prayer helps you turn to Him before deciding and moving forward.

5
When to Pray This Prayer

Pray this when you are facing a decision and do not know what to do. When the right choice is unclear, this prayer helps you pause and seek His advice and direction.

Pray this when you feel pressured to decide quickly. Instead of reacting ask God to give you clarity, understanding, and the will to act.

Pray this at the beginning of your day. Invite God's wisdom to guide your thoughts and formulate your decisions.

5
Wisdom Comes From You

Proverbs 2:6

Lord,
You are the source of wisdom.
Give me understanding that comes from You. Help me seek Your truth above my own ideas. Guide me in what is right.
Amen.

Your Word Guides Me

Psalm 119:105

Father,
Let Your Word guide my steps.
When I feel uncertain give me direction. Help me follow what You have shown me. Lead me forward in Your truth.
Amen.

5
Reflect and Respond

What decisions are you facing right now that feel unclear or difficult? Identify where you need wisdom most.

Are you relying more on your own desires and understanding or are you seeking God's direction? Be honest about your situation.

Bring that decision before God today. Ask Him for clarity and be willing to follow where He leads you.

5
Fill Me With Understanding

Colossians 1:9

Lord,
Fill me with the knowledge of Your will. Give me spiritual wisdom and understanding. Help me see clearly what You want for my life. Guide my decisions according to Your purpose.
Amen.

Show Me Your Ways

Psalm 25:4–5

Father,
Show me the path You have for me. Teach me Your ways and lead me in truth. Help me trust Your direction. Guide me as I walk in humble obedience.
Amen.

5
Reflect and Respond

Do you feel confident in the direction you are taking or are you uncertain? Consider whether you have truly sought God's wisdom.

What is one step you can take today to invite God into your decision-making process? Be specific.

Ask God to guide you and remain open to His continuing direction, even if it leads somewhere unexpected.

5
Live This Today

Before making a particular decision today, pause and ask God for wisdom. Even in small choices choose to seek His direction first.

God does not withhold wisdom from those who ask. As you turn to Him consistently, you will begin to recognize His guidance and grow in confidence in the path He is setting before you.

SECTION 6

Renewing Your Mind

6
Transformational Prayer

Renewing Your Mind

Father,
my thoughts often drift toward worry,
distraction, and what is untrue.
I replay things in my mind that pull me
away from You.
Renew my mind and reshape how I
think.
Replace what is false with Your truth
so my life begins to change.
Amen.

Memory Prayer:
Lord, renew my mind with Your truth.

6
Transformational Prayer

Scripture

Romans 12:2

"...be transformed by the
renewing of your mind..."

6
Why This Prayer Matters

Your thoughts quietly shape your life. What you dwell on influences how you feel, how you respond, and even the direction you take.

Left unchecked your mind can drift toward negativity or distraction. Over time these unwanted patterns begin to define your perspective and determine your choices.

God offers something different. He renews your mind so you begin to see clearly and think in alignment with truth. This prayer invites change which will help your thinking so your life can move in a new direction.

6
When to Pray This Prayer

Pray this when your thoughts are negative or overwhelming. When your mind is filled with worry or distraction, this prayer helps you refocus.

Pray this when outside influences begin to influence your thinking. When you feel pulled in different directions, ask God to refine your perspective.

Pray this at the start of your day. Invite God to shape your thoughts before anything else takes hold in your life.

6
Renew My Thinking

Ephesians 4:23

Lord,
Renew my mind from within.
Change how I think and respond.
Replace old patterns with Your truth.
Help me live with a new perspective.
Amen.

Set My Mind on What Matters

Colossians 3:2

Father,
Help me focus on what is true and lasting. Lift my thoughts above distractions. Guide my mind toward what honors You. Keep my attention centered on You.
Amen.

6
Reflect and Respond

What thoughts have been shaping your mindset recently? Examine your life and determine what has been guiding your decisions.

Are there patterns in your thinking that need to shift or change? Identify one specific area you want to improve.

Ask God to begin renewing your mind in that area. Be willing to replace your thoughts with His truth and allow Him to refocus how you think.

6
Open My Eyes to Your Truth

Psalm 119:18

God,
Open my eyes to understand Your truth. Help me see clearly what You are teaching me. Remove confusion and distraction. Let Your Word guide my thoughts.
Amen.

Let My Thoughts Please You

Psalm 19:14

Lord,
Let my thoughts be pleasing to You. Guard my mind from what is not right. Help me examine my thinking and my words. I want to reflect Your truth in all I do.
Amen.

6
Reflect and Respond

Do your thoughts reflect God's truth or the worldly pressures around you? Consider what has been influencing your thinking.

What is one thought pattern you need to change today? Be specific and write it down

Ask God to help you see and understand clearly. Examine and reshape your thoughts. As your thinking changes your life will begin to change as well.

6
Live This Today

When you notice your thoughts drifting today, pause and turn your attention back to God. Replace those thoughts with something true and life-giving.

You do not have to remain stuck in old patterns of thinking. God is able to renew your mind and reshape your perspective.

As you bring your thoughts to Him, you will begin to experience clarity, peace, and a new way of living.

SECTION 7

Becoming Like Christ

7
Transformational Prayer

Becoming Like Christ

Lord Jesus,
I want to become like You, but I keep returning to old habits.
I change outwardly, but my heart often stays the same.
Transform me from within.
Shape my thoughts and attitudes so my life reflects You more clearly.
Amen.

Memory Prayer:
Lord, make me more like You.

7
Transformational Prayer

Scripture

Romans 8:29
"...to be conformed to the
image of His Son..."

Galatians 4:19
"...until Christ is formed in you."

7
Why This Prayer Matters

Most people want to grow but real change is harder than it seems. You may recognize patterns in your life that need to shift, yet find yourself returning to the same responses.

God's purpose is not surface improvement. It is transformation. He is shaping you into the likeness of Christ, forming His character within you over time. This kind of change reaches deeper than behavior.

As Christlikeness is formed in you, your attitudes begin to shift and your reactions change. Your life will start to reflect Him and His character more clearly. This prayer invites God to do that deeper work in you.

7
When to Pray This Prayer

Pray this when you notice patterns in your life that do not reflect Christ. When the same struggle is repeated, this prayer helps you invite real change.

Pray this when your actions do not match with your desire to follow the Lord. In moments of frustration or weakness, ask Him to reshape your responses.

Pray this regularly as part of your growth. Transformation happens over time as you consistently invite God to form His character in you.

7
Transform Me as I Follow You

2 Corinthians 3:18

Lord,
As I turn toward You, change me. Transform me from the inside out. Help me reflect Your character more clearly. Make me more like You each day. Amen.

Shape My Attitude

Philippians 2:5

Father,
Give me the mindset of Christ. When I think selfishly, redirect my heart. Teach me humility and obedience. Help me respond the way Jesus would.
Amen.

7
Reflect and Respond

Where do you see a gap between your life and the character of Christ? Be open about one specific area where change is needed.

What pattern keeps repeating, even though you want it to change? Consider why it may still have a hold on you.

Bring that area before God today. Ask Him to reshape your heart and mind at a deeper level.

7
Renew Me in Your Image

Colossians 3:10

Lord,
Renew me from within.
Make me new in the way I think and live. Shape my life to reflect Your image. Help me grow into who You want me to be.
Amen.

Help Me Walk as You Walked

1 John 2:6

Lord Jesus,
Help me live the way You lived.
Guide my steps and my choices.
When I am unsure, show me how to follow You. Teach me to walk in Your ways daily.
Amen.

7
Reflect and Respond

If someone watched your life closely, what would they observe? Will they see your habits or Christ's character? Consider that seriously.

What is one response or attitude you want to change today? Be specific about how that would look.

Ask God to begin molding that area of your life. As you follow His leading, He will continue developing His character in you.

7
Live This Today

Before responding in a conversation today, pause and ask, "What would it look like to respond like Christ right now?" Then choose that response.

You are not expected to change fully or instantly. God is patiently and slowly transforming you into the nature of Christ.

As you take small intentional steps, you will begin to see real change in how you think, respond, and relate to Jesus.

SECTION 8

Living a Holy Life

8
Transformational Prayer

Living a Holy Life

Father,
I know what is right, but I often choose what pulls me away from You.
I excuse small compromises and ignore what needs to change.
Cleanse my heart and strengthen my resolve.
Help me turn from what is wrong and choose what honors You.
Amen.

Memory Prayer:
Lord, make my life holy.

8
Transformational Prayer

Scripture

1 Thessalonians 4:3

"It is God's will that you
should be sanctified…"

8
Why This Prayer Matters

Most people do not fall or rebel all at once—they drift slowly. Small compromises, poor choices, and repeated habits quietly shape the direction of your life.

What once felt wrong can begin to feel normal. Without realizing it your standards shift and your sensitivity fades or vanishes.

God calls you to something higher. He calls you to live a life that reflects His character, not the worldly values around you.

This prayer helps you turn back, realign your choices, and pursue a life that honors Him.

8
When to Pray This Prayer

Pray this when you become aware of habits or patterns that do not honor God. When something feels out of alignment, this prayer helps you turn back toward Him.

Pray this when you feel the pull of temptation. In moments where compromise seems easier, ask God to strengthen your resolve to stand fast.

Pray this at the end of your day. Reflect on your choices and invite God to shape your life more fully.

8
Create a Clean Heart

Psalm 51:10

God,
Create in me a clean heart.
Remove what is not right within me.
Renew my desire to follow You.
Help me live with honesty before You.
Amen.

Set Me Apart

1 Peter 1:15–16

Lord,
You have called me to be holy.
Help me live differently from what is around me. Transform my choices and my conduct. Let my life reflect Your character.
Amen.

8
Reflect and Respond

Are there areas in your life where you have become comfortable with what you know is not right? Be fully truthful in your self-evaluation.

What small compromise has begun to shape your habits or thinking? Identify something specific.

Bring your concerns before God today. Tell Him you want to change. Ask Him to create a clean heart and give you the strength to make a different choice moving forward.

8
Help Me Pursue What Is Right

Hebrews 12:14

Father,
Help me pursue what is right and pure. Give me strength to walk in obedience. When I feel pulled in wrong directions, guide me back. Lead me toward a life that honors You.
Amen.

Establish My Life in Holiness

1 Thessalonians 3:12–13

Lord,
Grow my love and strengthen my heart. Establish me in holiness before You. Shape my life so it is steady and true. Help me live in a way that reflects You daily.
Amen.

8
Reflect and Respond

If someone observed your daily choices what patterns would they notice? Would they see a life moving toward God or drifting away?

Where do you need to take a clear step toward holiness today?

Ask God to strengthen your heart and guide your choices. As you respond, He will shape your life in the right direction.

8
Live This Today

When you face a small choice today, think about whether it leads you toward or away from God? Then choose what honors Him.

Holiness is built through small consistent decisions. You do not change all at once, but each step does matter.

As you choose what is right, God is shaping your life into something stronger and more aligned with His ways.

SECTION 9

Loving Others

9
Transformational Prayer

Loving Others

Lord,
I know You call me to love others, but
I struggle under certain circumstances.
When I feel hurt or frustrated my heart
closes up.
Time has built up barriers and it has
become hard for me.
Help me respond with patience,
humility, and compassion—even in the
most trying circumstances.
Amen.

Memory Prayer:
Lord, empower me to love others.

9
Transformational Prayer

Scripture

John 13:34

"Love one another.
As I have loved you…"

9
Why This Prayer Matters

Loving others sounds simple. But relationships can become difficult. Tension, disappointment, or past hurt can impact how you respond to people.

Jesus has set a high standard. He calls you to love others the way He loves you: with sacrifice and patience. This kind of love response does not depend on how others treat you.

Left on your own, your love will often be limited by your feelings. But as God molds your heart, your responses begin to reflect His ways more than your personal preferences. This prayer helps you reflect God's love.

9
When to Pray This Prayer

Pray this when you feel frustration rising toward someone. When irritation begins to shape your words, pause and bring it before God.

Pray this when you are holding onto hurt. Instead of letting it grow, ask God to soften your heart.

Pray this before difficult conversations. Invite God to guide your attitude so your words and actions reflect His love.

9
Strengthen Me in Love

Ephesians 3:16–19

Father,
Strengthen me in my inner being.
Center my life deeply in Your love.
Help me understand how great Your love is. Fill my heart so I can love others well.
Amen.

Make Me Kind and Forgiving

Ephesians 4:32

Lord,
Make me kind in how I respond.
When I feel hurt help me choose forgiveness. Remove harshness from my words and actions. Teach me to treat others with grace.
Amen.

9
Reflect and Respond

Who is the person you find hardest to love right now? What specifically makes it difficult?

Have you allowed frustration or hurt to determine how you treat them? Consider a recent interaction and how you might have responded better.

What is one specific way you could respond differently next time? Ask God to help you act with kindness, even if your feelings have not caught up to your intent yet.

9
Help Me Put Others First

Philippians 2:3–4

Father,
When I focus on myself, shift my attention outward. Help me value others above my own comfort.
Teach me to notice their needs.
Give me a willing heart to serve others.
Amen.

Increase My Love Daily

1 Thessalonians 3:12

Lord,
Grow my love beyond what it is today.
Do not let it remain shallow or conditional. Expand my capacity to care for others. Help my love increase and overflow.
Amen.

9
Reflect and Respond

If someone experienced your love this week, what would they say it felt like? Would they describe goodness and kindness or impatience and tension?

When do you tend to put your own comfort or preferences ahead of others? Identify one specific situation.

Ask God to increase your love in a visible way. What is one simple act you could do today that would put someone else first?

9
Live This Today

Choose one person today and take a specific action to show them love. Send a message, offer encouragement, or do something that serves them.

Love grows through action, not just thoughts or intention.

As you take small steps to care for others, God expands your heart and shapes how you live.

SECTION 10

Strength in Trials

10
Transformational Prayer

Strength in Trials

Lord,
when life is difficult, I tend to want relief more than growth.
I grow tired and lose perspective.
Strengthen me from within and help me endure. Allow me to trust You in trials, and remain strong when I feel worn down.
Amen.

Memory Prayer:
Lord, strengthen my endurance.

10
Transformational Prayer

Scripture

Colossians 1:11
"...being strengthened... so that you may have endurance and patience."

James 1:2–4
"...the testing of your faith produces perseverance..."

10
Why This Prayer Matters

When life becomes difficult, your first instinct may be to escape the problems. You may want relief, answers, or change, and you probably want it now.

But trials are not meaningless. God uses them to build endurance, strengthen your faith, or shape your character in ways comfort never could.

When you begin to pray for strength, instead of only relief, your perspective will shift. You are no longer just trying to get through a trial, you are asking God to work on you within it. This prayer helps you endure with purpose.

10
When to Pray This Prayer

Pray this when you feel overwhelmed or emotionally drained. When your strength feels depleted, bring that feeling before God.

Pray this when you are tempted to give up. Ask God to steady you in moments where continuing feels challenging.

Pray this during long seasons of uncertainty. When answers are delayed, invite God to build endurance and patience in you.

10
Strength Through Struggle

Romans 5:3–5

Father,
When I face hardship, help me face what You are doing in my life. Build perseverance in me through this difficulty. Shape my character in ways comfort cannot. Let hope and faith grow stronger in me.
Amen.

Your Grace Is Enough

2 Corinthians 12:9

Lord,
When I feel weak, remind me that Your grace is enough. Meet me in my limitations. Show Your strength in my weakness. Help me depend on You.
Amen.

10
Reflect and Respond

Where are you currently feeling stretched beyond your strength? Be specific about your feelings and fears.

Have you been asking only for the trial to end, or do you need strength to endure it well?

What would it look like to respond with confidence instead of frustration today? Ask God to help you take some steps forward.

10
My Refuge in Trouble

Psalm 46:1

God,
You are my refuge and strength.
When everything feels unstable, help me come to You first. Be present with me in this trouble. Remind me that I am not alone.
Amen.

Restore and Strengthen Me

1 Peter 5:10

Father,
After this season restore what has been worn down. Strengthen and establish my life. Use this trial to make me more steadfast. Help me trust that You are at work in my life.
Amen.

10
Reflect and Respond

When pressure and tension increase, where do you instinctively turn? Are you seeking God's favor or are you turning away to other alternatives?

What has this trial revealed about your endurance, resilience, and your dependence on God?

Ask Him to become your first place of refuge. What would change if you brought your struggle to Him today?

10
Live This Today

When stress occurs or life pressures rise, pause and ask God to strengthen you in that moment. Then move forward one step at a time. Don't look too far ahead.

Endurance is built in small increments built up over time. You do not need strength for the whole journey. You just need His helping hand for what is in front of you right now.

SECTION 11

Living With Eternal Perspective

11
Transformational Prayer

Eternal Perspective

Father,
I can get consumed by what feels urgent and tend to lose sight of what really matters.
I often focus on what is temporary instead of what is eternal.
Lift my thoughts beyond today.
Help me see my life from Your perspective and live with what matters most in view.
Amen.

Memory Prayer:
Lord, help me recognize what has eternal significance.

11
Transformational Prayer

Scripture

Colossians 3:1–2

"...set your hearts on things above...
not on earthly things."

11
Why This Prayer Matters

The things that feel urgent today can quickly lose their importance tomorrow. Daily pressures have a way of filling your thoughts and narrowing your focus.

If you are not careful, you can spend your energy chasing what is temporary, while neglecting what truly matters. Much of what consumes your attention will not last.

God invites you to live with a different perspective. When your focus shifts beyond the visible and immediate, your priorities begin to change. This prayer helps you step back, refocus, and align your life with what has eternal significance.

11
When to Pray This Prayer

Pray this when daily pressures begin to crowd out what matters most. When everything feels urgent, ask God to help you step back and see clearly.

Pray this when you are making decisions about time, priorities or you're your future direction. Invite God to guide you toward what matters instead of what is merely immediate.

Pray this when you feel discouraged or stuck. Ask God to help you discern what is temporary and what is eternal.

11
Invest in What Lasts

Matthew 6:19–21

Father,
Help me not to invest my life in what will fade. Turn my attention toward what is lasting. Cause my heart to value what You value. Teach me to invest in what endures.
Amen.

Fix My Eyes Beyond Today

2 Corinthians 4:18

Lord,
When I am consumed by what I can see, lift my eyes higher. Help me focus on what has eternal significance. Keep me from being defined by temporary circumstances. Anchor my perspective in what truly lasts.
Amen.

11
Reflect and Respond

What is currently consuming most of your attention and energy? Will it still matter a year from now?

Where have temporary worldly pressures begun to shape your priorities? Identify what is really driving your decisions.

What would change if you truly lived focused on what is eternal? Identify one change you want to make today.

11
Remember Where I Belong

Philippians 3:20

Father,
Remind me that my true citizenship is in heaven. Keep me from becoming too attached to what is temporary. Help me live as someone who belongs to something greater. Form my life around that identity.
Amen.

Teach Me to Number My Days

Psalm 90:12

Lord,
Teach me to see the value of each day. Help me live with wisdom and intention. Do not let me waste what You have given me. Guide me to use my time in ways that matter.
Amen.

11
Reflect and Respond

If your life continues exactly as it is, where will your current focus lead you? Consider the direction your current choices are taking you.

Are you investing more in what is temporary or what is eternal? Identify where your time and energy are being spent. What's important to you?

Ask God to realign your perspective. What is one decision you can make today that would reflect what truly matters in your life?

11
Live This Today

Before making a decision today ask, "Will this matter in light of eternity?" Let the answer shape your response, even in small choices.

A life shaped by eternal perspectives does not ignore today, but rather gives today its proper place.

As you focus on what has eternal significance, your priorities become clearer and your decisions more focused and intentional.

SECTION 12

Finishing Faithfully

12
Transformational Prayer

Finishing Faithfully

Lord,
I begin with good intentions, but I do not always stay on track.
I tend to become distracted, tired, and I lose focus over time.
Strengthen my resolve to remain faithful.
Help me endure through difficulties, and finish this life well.
Amen.

Memory Prayer:
Lord, help me finish faithfully.

12
Transformational Prayer

Scripture

2 Timothy 4:7

"I have fought the good fight,
I have finished the race,
I have kept the faith."

12
Why This Prayer Matters

Many people begin with clarity and conviction but over time they get side-tracked. Life is not only about how you start, it's also about how you finish.

Discouragement, frustration, and apathy can slowly pull you off course. What once felt important can become secondary. Focus and consistency can begin to fade. Without intentionality it is easy to drift.

God calls you to a life marked by endurance and faithfulness. This prayer helps you stay anchored and steadfast so that when your journey is complete, you can look back knowing you remained faithful.

12
When to Pray This Prayer

Pray this prayer when your focus begins to slip. When what once mattered deeply starts losing priority, ask God to realign your heart to what matters most.

Pray this when you feel tired or discouraged. In seasons when progress feels slow, ask God to strengthen your patience and perseverance.

Pray this when you face long-term responsibilities or commitments. Invite God to help you remain focused so you can finish well.

12
Help Me Run with Endurance

Hebrews 12:1–2

Father,
Help me lay aside what slows me down.
Give me endurance to keep going.
Fix my eyes on what truly matters.
Keep me moving forward with purpose.
Amen.

Complete What You Began in Me

Philippians 1:6

Lord,
You began a good work in me.
Do not let me abandon it halfway.
Continue shaping and growing my life.
Bring Your work in me to completion.
Amen.

12
Reflect and Respond

Where have you lost intentionality in something that once mattered deeply? Identify a specific area, not just a general feeling.

What has caused you to drift? Are you discouraged or frustrated? Be real about the root causes.

What would it look like to re-engage with intention today? Ask God to help you take one meaningful step back toward faithfulness.

12
Help Me Run to Win

1 Corinthians 9:24

Father,
Do not let me live without purpose. Help me run with focus and discipline. Give me the determination to stay the course. Teach me to pursue what truly matters.
Amen.

Keep Me Faithful to the End

Revelation 2:10

Lord,
Help me remain faithful no matter the cost. When challenges arise, strengthen my resolve. Keep my heart steady and committed to You. Lead me to endure all the way to the end.
Amen.

12
Reflect and Respond

If your current patterns continue, will they lead you to finish well? Consider the direction your life is actually going, not just your intentions.

Where are you tempted to give less effort or attention to your faith than you once did? Have you lost your interest or intensity?

Ask God to renew your commitment. What is one area where you need to return to faithfulness starting today?

12
Live This Today

Choose one commitment today that you will follow through on consistently. Take a clear step forward today.

Faithfulness is built through positive daily decisions. You do not finish well by accident. You remain faithful by staying steadfast and obedient each and every day.

When you choose consistency today, you are shaping a life that will endure to the end.

12 Faith Goals That Will Transform Your Life

<u>I want:</u>

1 God to be the driving force of my life!

2 to be overwhelmed by His acts of power, mighty deeds, and surpassing greatness.

3 to have a consuming passion for God.

4 my heart and soul to be occupied with God.

5 the will/power to exalt and proclaim His Name.

6 an intensified awareness of His presence.

7 to bring glory to His Name.

8 to abide in His grace, love, and wisdom.

9 a deep personal hunger for His Word.

10 to love God completely – heart, body and soul.

11 to be obsessed with imitating Christ.

12 live worthy of a child of God.

12 Life-Changing Discipleship Commitment Prayers

1 Righteousness: Fill me with Your righteousness that I might be blameless in Your sight.
2 Mercy and Compassion: Remove all selfishness and pride; fill me with mercy and compassion.
3 Humility: Enable me to walk humbly in the path You have set before me.
4 Truth: Teach me to know right from wrong and act accordingly.
5 Gratitude: Enable me to express gratitude and joy in every situation.
6 Uplifting Speech: Guard my tongue so that my speech is true, helpful, and uplifting.
7 Worship: I want to glorify You every day in all I do and say. Bless me with a life of true worship.
8 For Confession and Repentance: Lord, give me the courage to openly confess my faults and trespasses and turn away from sin.
9 Obedience: Give me courage to carry out Your will for my life, living in obedience to Your Word.
10 Serving: May all I do be done as unto Christ. Allow me to find joy in all tasks that serve others.
11 Love: I want to love You and others as I do myself, being kind, trustworthy, and faithful.
12 Praise: Help me to offer You a continual sacrifice of praise for You are worthy of worship.

The Wisdom Prayer Series

Personal Prayer Guide

Prayer Resource and Journal

This is a great resource to kick-start your prayer life!

Know what to pray.
Pray based on Bible verses.
Strengthen your prayer life.
Access reference resources.
Pray with eternal implications.
Write your own prayers if desired.
Organize and focus your prayer time.
Learn what the Bible says about prayer.
Find encouragement and advice on how to pray.
Reduce frustration in your prayer time.

Get your copy today!

https://www.amazon.com/dp/1952359260

The Wisdom Prayer Series

Are You Walking With Jesus

Devotional

Are You Walking With Jesus is designed to support a steady and thoughtful rhythm of discipleship rather than a hurried reading plan. The goal is to allow prayer, Scripture, and reflection to shape your devotional life for 60 days.

This devotional invites you to consider a simple but life-shaping question: *Are you walking with Jesus?* Over the next sixty days, these prayers and reflections are designed to help you deepen your relationship with Christ, align your heart with His will, and live each day in faithful discipleship.

https://www.amazon.com/dp/1952359791

The Wisdom Prayer Series

Prayers of Eternal Significance

You do not need to pray more words!
You need to pray with purpose, and eternal focus.

- Learn how to pray with eternal priorities.
- Refocus your prayer life around God's will.
- Discover prayers that shape decisions and daily direction.
- Pray with focus and meaning.
- Pray for spiritual growth, wisdom, and transformation.
- Strengthen your relationship with God.
- Pray for others with greater depth and eternal perspective.
- Discover transformational life-shaping prayer.
- Develop lasting and substantial prayer patterns.
- Prayers aligned with what matters most to you.

https://www.amazon.com/dp/195235983X

About the Author

After 25 years as an actuary, and 20 years as an entrepreneur, Steve began his third career as an author in 2020. He published *The OBSCURE Bible Study Series* in 2020 and the *The Jesus Follower Bible Study Series* in 2024. He is a member of The Church at Station Hill in Spring Hill, TN, a regional campus of Brentwood Baptist.

This prayer book came about when Steve decided to publish The Wisdom Prayer Series.

www.getwisdompublishing.com

Contact Information

Get Wisdom – General Information

www.getwisdompublishing.com

The Wisdom Prayer Series

Resource: "What Should I Pray?"

Devotional: "Are You Walking With Jesus?"

Prayer: "Can prayer Change Your Life?"

https://www.amazon.com/dp/B0GX31YV7f

OBSCURE Bible Study Series

https://www.amazon.com/dp/B08T7TL1B1

Jesus Follower Bible Study Series

https://www.amazon.com/dp/B0DHP39P5J

The Life Planning Series

https://www.amazon.com/dp/B09TH9SYC4

NOTE: You Can Help!

Please leave an honest review on
the Amazon Sales Page:
https://www.amazon.com/dp/1952359813

GETWISDOM
PUBLISHING

GETWISDOM
PUBLISHING

www.ingramcontent.com/pod-product-compliance
Lightning Source LLC
LaVergne TN
LVHW051005080826
845145LV00009B/2473

* 9 7 8 1 9 5 2 3 5 9 8 1 1 *